Talking into the Ear of a Donkey

Also by Robert Bly

POETRY

Reaching Out to the World:
New and Selected Prose Poems

My Sentence Was a Thousand Years of Joy

The Urge to Travel Long Distances

The Night Abraham Called to the Stars

The Insanity of Empire:
A Book of Poems Against the Iraq War

Eating the Honey of Words: New and Selected Poems

Morning Poems

Meditations on the Insatiable Soul

What Have I Ever Lost by Dying?:
Collected Prose Poems

Angels of Pompeii
(with Stephen Brigidi)

Selected Poems

Loving a Woman in Two Worlds

The Man in the Black Coat Turns

This Tree Will Be Here for a Thousand Years

Old Man Rubbing His Eyes

This Body Is Made of Camphor and Gopherwood

Jumping Out of Bed

Sleepers Joining Hands

The Light Around the Body

Silence in the Snowy Fields

PROSE

The Maiden King
(with Marion Woodman)

The Sibling Society

Remembering James Wright

Iron John

American Poetry: Wildness and Domesticity

A Little Book on the Human Shadow
(with William Booth)

Talking All Morning

Eight Stages of Translation

Talking into the Ear of a Donkey

Poems

Robert Bly

W. W. Norton & Company

New York • London

For information about permission to reproduce selections from
this book, write to Permissions, W. W. Norton & Company, Inc.,
500 Fifth Avenue, New York, NY 10110

For information about special discounts for bulk purchases,
please contact W. W. Norton Special Sales at
specialsales@wwnorton.com or 800-233-4830

Manufacturing by Courier Westford
Book design by Lovedog Studio
Production manager: Devon Zahn

Library of Congress Cataloging-in-Publication Data

Bly, Robert.
Talking into the ear of a donkey :
poems / Robert Bly. — 1st ed.
      p. cm.
ISBN 978-0-393-08022-3 (hardcover)
I. Title.
PS3552.L9T35 2011
811'.54—dc22

                                        2010052448

W. W. Norton & Company, Inc.,
500 Fifth Avenue, New York, NY 10110
www.wwnorton.com

W. W. Norton & Company, Ltd.,
75/76 Wells Street, London W1T 3QT

1 2 3 4 5 6 7 8 9 0

Contents

Two

Three

Four

Five

Six

Acknowledgments

Some of these poems appeared in the following publications, sometimes in earlier versions or under different titles. Thanks to the editors for permission to reprint them: *Alaska Quarterly Review; American Poetry Review; Atlantic Monthly; The Bitter Oleander; Chokecherries; The Evansville Review; Five Points; Great River Review; Grey Sparrow Journal; Knockout; Lips; Mobius; Otter Tail Review; Parabola; The Paris Review; Poetrybay* (online); *Poetry Northwest; Speakeasy; Water-Stone.*

These poems originally appeared in *Poetry*: "Longing for the Acrobat" (as "Living at the End of the World"); "Ravens Hiding in a Shoe."

The following originally appeared in *The New Yorker*: "Courting Forgetfulness"; "Heard Whispers"; "I Have Daughters and I Have Sons"; "A Poetry Reading at Benedictine College in Atchison, Kansas"; "Sunday Afternoon"; "Turkish Pears in August"; "Wanting Sumptuous Heavens."

The following originally appeared in *Poetry East*: "My Father at Forty"; "The Man at the Door."

"The Mourning Dove's Call" was first published in the anthology *It Has Come to This*; "The Old Fishing Lines" was first published in *The Chrysalis Reader: Passages*; "Something to Do for Aunt Clara" first appeared in the *Sourcebooks Poetry Calendar 2009*; "Starting a Poem" first appeared in the *Alhambra Poetry Calendar 2010* (Belgium).

An early version of "Talking into the Ear of a Donkey" appeared in *Eating the Honey of Words: New and Selected Poems*, HarperCollins, 1999.

Talking into the Ear of a Donkey

One

_____

Ravens Hiding in a Shoe

There is something men and women living in houses
Don't understand. The old alchemists standing
Near their stoves hinted at it a thousand times.

Ravens at night hide in an old woman's shoe.
A four-year-old speaks some ancient language.
We have lived our own death a thousand times.

Each sentence we speak to friends means the opposite
As well. Each time we say, "I trust in God," it means
God has already abandoned us a thousand times.

Mothers again and again have knelt in church
In wartime asking God to protect their sons,
And their prayers were refused a thousand times.

The baby loon follows the mother's sleek
Body for months. By the end of summer, she
Has dipped her head into Rainy Lake a thousand times.

Robert, you've wasted so much of your life
Sitting indoors to write poems. Would you
Do that again? I would, a thousand times.

Courting Forgetfulnesss

It's hard to know what sort of rough music
Could send our forgetfulness back into the ground,
From which the gravediggers pulled it years ago.

The first moment of the day we court forgetfulness.
Even when we are fully awake, a century can
Go by in the space of a single heartbeat.

The life we lose through forgetfulness resembles
The earth that sticks to the sides of plowshares
And the eggs the hen has abandoned in the woods.

A thousand gifts were given to us in the womb.
We lost hundreds during the forgetfulness of birth,
And we lost the old heaven on the first day of school.

Forgetfulness resembles the snow that weighs down
The fir boughs; behind our house you'll find
A forest going on for hundreds of miles.

It's to our credit that we can remember
So many lines of Rilke, but the purpose of forgetfulness
Is to remember the last time we left this world.

Keeping Our Small Boat Afloat

So many blessings have been given to us
During the first distribution of light, that we are
Admired in a thousand galaxies for our grief.

Don't expect us to appreciate creation or to
Avoid mistakes. Each of us is a latecomer
To the earth, picking up wood for the fire.

Every night another beam of light slips out
From the oyster's closed eye. So don't give up hope
That the door of mercy may still be open.

Seth and Shem, tell me, are you still grieving
Over the spark of light that descended with no
Defender near into the Egypt of Mary's womb?

It's hard to grasp how much generosity
Is involved in letting us go on breathing,
When we contribute nothing valuable but our grief.

Each of us deserves to be forgiven, if only for
Our persistence in keeping our small boat afloat
When so many have gone down in the storm.

Paying Attention to the Melody

All right. I know that each of us will die alone.
It doesn't matter how loud or soft the sitar plays.
Sooner or later the melody will say it all.

The prologue is so long! At last the theme comes.
It says the soul will rise above all these notes.
It says the dust will be swept up from the floor.

It doesn't matter if we say our prayers or not.
We know the canoe is heading straight for the falls,
And no one will pick us up from the water this time.

One day the mice will carry our ragged impulses
All the way to Egypt, and at home the cows
Will graze on a thousand acres of thought.

Everyone goes on hoping for a good death.
The old rope hangs down from the hangman's nail.
The forty-nine robbers are climbing into their boots.

Robert, don't expect too much. You've put yourself
Ahead of others for years, a hundred years.
It will take a long time for you to hear the melody.

Longing for the Acrobat

There is so much sweetness in children's voices,
And so much discontent at the end of day,
And so much satisfaction when a train goes by.

I don't know why the rooster keeps on crying,
Nor why the elephant lifts his knobby trunk,
Nor why Hawthorne kept hearing trains at night.

A handsome child is a gift from God,
And a friend is a vein in the back of the hand,
And a wound is an inheritance from the wind.

Some say we are living at the end of time,
But I believe a thousand pagan ministers
Will arrive tomorrow to baptize the wind.

There's nothing we need to do about Saint John.
Whenever he laid his hands on earth
The well water was sweet for a hundred miles.

Everywhere people are longing for a deeper life.
Let's hope some acrobat will come by
And give us a hint how to get into heaven.

Nirmala's Music

The music that Nirmala is playing today goes
By two names: The One Who Finds Lost Things,
And The One Through Whom Everything Is Lost.

Tigers go on eating people in the Forest
Of Existence. The gods agree to this. Saints
Admire whiskers that have been dipped in blood.

Women with their newly washed hair, the souls
Born again and again into sleek, fresh bodies,
Boards leaning against a barn . . . what does it all mean?

Men think ahead, and are mainly providential.
They laid out Egypt. But I like women so much.
They say: "Let the lambs come and be killed."

And women suffer the most. Between every child born,
So many rugs are woven and taken apart. The water
Of a hundred bowls is poured out on the ground.

The hungry tigers follow the disappearing dogs
Into the woods of life. Women understand this,
For this is a world in which everything is lost.

The Frogs After Dark

I am so much in love with mournful music
That I don't bother to look for violinists.
The aging peepers satisfy me for hours.

The ant moves on his tiny Sephardic feet.
The flute is always glad to repeat the same note.
The ocean rejoices in its dusky mansion.

Bears are often piled up close to each other.
In caves of bears, it's just one hump
After another, and there is no one to sort it out.

You and I have spent so many hours working.
We have paid dearly for the life we have.
It's all right if we do nothing tonight.

We've heard the fiddlers tuning their old fiddles,
And the singer urging the low notes to come.
We've heard her trying to keep the dawn from breaking.

There is some slowness in life that is right for us.
But we love to remember the way the soul leaps
Over and over into the lonely heavens.

The Sympathies of the
Long Married

Oh well, let's go on eating the grains of eternity.
What do we care about improvements in travel?
Angels sometimes cross the river on old turtles.

Shall we worry about who gets left behind?
That one bird flying through the clouds is enough.
Your sweet face at the door of the house is enough.

The two farm horses stubbornly pull the wagon.
The mad crows carry away the tablecloth.
Most of the time, we live through the night.

Let's not drive the wild angels from our door.
Maybe the mad fields of grain will move.
Maybe the troubled rocks will learn to walk.

It's all right if we're troubled by the night.
It's all right if we can't recall our own name.
It's all right if this rough music keeps on playing.

I've given up worrying about men living alone.
I do worry about the couple who live next door.
Some words heard through the screen door are enough.

The Blind Old Man

I don't know why so much sweetness hovers around us,
Nor why the wind blows the curtains in the afternoons,
Nor why the earth mutters so much about its children.

We'll never know why the snow falls through the night,
Nor how the heron stretches her long legs,
Nor why we feel so abandoned in the morning.

We have never understood how birds manage to fly,
Nor who the genius is who makes up dreams,
Nor how heaven and earth can appear in a poem.

We don't know why the rain falls so long.
The ditchdigger turns up one shovel after another.
The herons go on stitching the heavens together.

We've never heard about the day we were conceived,
Nor the doctor who helped us to be born,
Nor that blind old man who decides when we will die.

It's hard to understand why the sun rises,
And why our children are mostly fond of us,
And why the wind blows the curtains in the afternoon.

Father and Son

There's no end to the going forth on ships,
And the clack of the dog's paws on the floor,
And women who are still lively at eighty.

There's no end to the rumbling of train cars,
And the whine of the twenty-year-old driver turning
The corner, and the dog barking to the end of time.

There's no end to the trampling of horses,
And the way old men throw down their cards,
And the haughty look on the opera singer's face.

There's no end to my ragged stanzas,
And the shirttails blowing in the wind,
And the tree branches broken in the storm.

Have I said there's no end to people dying,
To the drops of sweat on the young girl's shoulder,
And the fatigue of the threshing hands at dusk?

There's a way in which card games finally do end,
And the convict finally turns himself in,
And the father sends his youngest son off on the bus.

Two

Rains

The weather is moody and rainy.
No one knows when Jesus will come.
The long rains have come and gone.
A thousand acres are underwater.

The Roof Nail

A hundred boats are still looking for shore.
There is more in my hopes than I imagined.
The tiny roof nail lies on the ground, aching for the roof.
Some little bone in our foot is longing for heaven.

A Day in Late June

The old man sits in his chair and looks down.
It will come, my dears. The femur leads
To the kneecap, and New Zealand is not
Far behind. They will all catch up.

Schoolchildren are free. Curtains stretch
Out before the window like girls on a picnic.
None of the famous ones have died. The boys
Still hold in them the seeds of Roncevaux.

New people have taken over the motel. It's
All right. What right did we have to throw
Tires into the river? Plotinus nursed
Until he was eight. He saw the Dear One,

And she is the hardest to see. The hawk's
Wing feathers shine. His eyes are bright.
Some invisible sweetness holds the knee
And the kneecap together. Our tongue

Goes on moving; the fire in the heart
Continues burning. Sparkles of sunshine
Light up the curtains that sway in the wind.
The old man sits in his chair and looks down.

Dealing with Parents

It's hard to know what to say about parents:
One man said, "I failed my parents." He led his parents
Across a lousy street—two lines of traffic.
Another started a lost colony for his parents.
He rowed across the river, towing his parents.
He bought them boots and pith helmets,
And sent them into battle. One man dressed them
In Austrian uniforms and gave them
Maps of Russia. No one ever saw them again.
Another man who had studied alchemy
Tried to transubstantiate his parents. It used
A lot of heat but there wasn't much change.
Someone else I knew stored his parents
In an empty cistern—the ladder is still sticking out.
Another man tied his parents all one day
And night in a rocking chair. And they
Died all right. . . . But by the end, they
Knew for certain that they'd had children.

The Sense of Getting Older

There's no doubt winter is coming. I see
My London Fog jacket is made in China.
The fall is like a bare writing desk.
The ash tree outside my window
Has no leaves, and Ignatow is gone. . . .
But my pen still moves freely
On this paper. And Vera, where is she?
In a nursing home in Newtonville.
Lamplight shines on the floorboards.
No response. Can I read anything I want
Now, how about *Stalingrad*? Go ahead.
Those I am dear to, those dear to me . . .
I can stand and let my palms sweep
Up over my stomach furnace—
You know, the potbellied stove
The Taoists talk about. And maybe
A plume of energy does climb,
As they say, up the spine. The turtles
On the Galápagos don't feel old.
They breathe only once a minute.

The Old Fishing Lines

Sometimes I get in my car on a late October day
And drive north. Everything that I haven't done—
Raking, visiting—all those reasons for not living—
Fall away. I pass half-abandoned summer towns,
Admiring the shadows thrown by bare trees
On bare lakes where cold waves lap the sand.

The renegade minister—the one they all gossip
About—would see those waves too, after throwing
His Sunday hat out the window. He'll be
All right. Death hugs the underside of oak leaves.
In each cove you pass you will see
What you had to say no to once.

It's all right if you walk down to the shore.
You'll feel time passing, the way the summer has.
You'll see the little holes that raindrops leave in fine sand
And the old fishing lines driven up on the rocks.

Walking Out in the Morning

In the city, whenever you walk out,
The air hits you first . . . abundant,
Nonhuman. Where has it been?
It's like your first college course,

But with better teachers. Farther on,
Your legs begin to feel the cold.
And you learn more. It's like
Graduate school, in which

Your boots keep slipping on
The loose rock as you make
Your way upward through
The shale of the great poems.

If you keep walking anyway,
You'll soon be on top. You'll know
You've read a lot of Germans
When your boots are full of snow.

A Poetry Reading in Maryland

for Lucille Clifton

You'd have been surprised at lower Maryland.
This far south we could still sense Washington:
George's powdered hair in the shad blossoms,
So many criminals wanting pardon from Lincoln.
We all admired the great trees, leaning out over
The bay, the English grandeur in the wide lawns.

We came by train to read poems. All of us
Were carrying something—it was hard to say what:
Perhaps luck, or perhaps some recklessness
About truth, or perhaps just a few small stones
We kept in our pockets giving off a fragrance
The students didn't get enough of at home.

We confessed a little—we had to—having brought
So much that was hidden with us, but our intent
Was not to confess. Our intent was to shine a little,
Suggest that we had done well, and drop
A hint about our childhood in the hope that
We too would receive some sort of pardon.

The Lost Trapper

Each time the soprano and the tenor
Kneel and sing to each other,
Somewhere else on stage the baritone
Is about to die.

The Alaskan trapper finds
Blood on his arm, his radio
Dead, and new snow
Falling on the branches.

I don't know why the grasshopper
Doesn't try to wiggle
Out from the bird's claw,
But he doesn't move.

Just forget the idea that
Someone will come and save
You whenever cedars begin
Making that low sound.

Starting a Poem

You're alone. Then there's a knock
On the door. It's a word. You
Bring it in. Things go
OK for a while. But this word

Has relatives. Soon
They turn up. None of them work.
They sleep on the floor, and they steal
Your tennis shoes.

You started it; you weren't
Content to leave things alone.
Now the den is a mess, and the
Remote is gone.

That's what being married
Is like! You never receive your
Wife only, but the
Madness of her family.

Now see what's happened?
Where is your car? You won't
Be able to find
The keys for a week.

I Have Daughters and I Have Sons

1

Who is out there at six a.m.? The man
Throwing newspapers onto the porch,
And the roaming souls suddenly
Drawn down into their sleeping bodies.

2

Wild words of Jacob Böhme
Go on praising the human body,
But heavy words of the ascetics
Sway in the fall gales.

3

Do I have a right to my poems?
To my jokes? To my loves?
Oh foolish man, knowing nothing—
Less than nothing—about desire.

4

I have daughters and I have sons.
When one of them lays a hand
On my shoulder, shining fish
Turn suddenly in the deep sea.

5

At this age, I especially love dawn
On the sea, stars above the trees,
Pages in *The Threefold Life*,
And the pale faces of baby mice.

6

Perhaps our life is made of struts
And paper, like those early
Wright Brothers planes. Neighbors
Run along holding the wingtips.

7

I do love Yeats's fierceness
As he jumped into a poem,
And that lovely calm in my father's
Hands, as he buttoned his coat.

The Mourning Dove's Call

for Peggy and Frank

The mourning dove's call woke me
In the still night, when it was still night
To me. Those sounds were older even
Than the box radio, and they said,
"Your mother is walking along the road.
I saw your dead father last night
Near the cottonwood grove."
I slept all night in a house with dear
Friends asleep in a neighboring room.
The call woke me in the still night.

Talking into the Ear of a Donkey

I have been talking into the ear of a donkey.
I have so much to say! And the donkey can't wait
To feel my breath stirring the immense oats
Of his ears. "What has happened to the spring,"
I cry, "and our legs that were so joyful
In the bobblings of April?" "Oh, never mind
About all that," the donkey
Says. "Just take hold of my mane, so you
Can lift your lips closer to my hairy ears."

Wanting Sumptuous Heavens

No one grumbles among the oyster clans,
And lobsters play their bone guitars all summer.
Only we, with our opposable thumbs, want
Heaven to be, and God to come, again.
There is no end to our grumbling; we want
Comfortable earth *and* sumptuous heaven.
But the heron standing on one leg in the bog
Drinks his dark rum all day, and is content.

Three

A Family Thing

I guess it's an old family
Thing. Someone is Napoléon,
Someone is sacrificed. Call in
Jesus, if you don't get it.

Pick up that cookie on the floor.
Let the hired man go on
Wasting his life. He'll find
Someone to waste it with.

It's like a game in which
The game itself loses.
It's like a picnic in which
The basket eats the food.

It's all right if I go to college;
Most people don't. It's all right
To end up bringing your own
Father home. Just be quiet.

Some powers are stronger
Than we are. They never say
When the battle is.
It was last night. You lost.

The Water Tank

It's late fall, and the box-elder leaves are gone.
Snow falls on the horses among their hay bales
And on the water tank overturned for winter.
The horses bend their necks toward the white ground to eat.

The Box of Chocolates

He always knew where he had been, and he remembered
The box elder in the fence post, looked down on men
Who couldn't see the storm coming. He'd learned
To live with the way his bait went deeper.

My mother kept her spirits high with little jobs.
He bought her a heart-shaped box of chocolates
Once a year. One life, one woman,
That was God's rule, and he didn't like it much.

Keeping Quiet

A friend of mine says that every war
Is some violence in childhood coming closer.
Those whoppings in the shed weren't a joke.
On the whole, it didn't turn out well.

This has been going on for thousands
Of years! It doesn't change. Something
Happened to me, and I can't tell
Anyone, so it will happen to you.

The Day the Dock Comes In

So much happens when the dock comes in.
Oak leaves are underfoot. They crackle
As we carry oars to the newly painted shed.
The lake is explaining its early life.

My four hanging apples are gone, I don't
Know where. Little adjustments are every-
Where. We'll have to get ready to read
Seneca—the bookcase will explain.

It's time now to pull up the posts,
Drag the dock in, pile the sections,
Lift the boat on top, and see how
Much subtlety is lost in explaining things.

Morning Pajamas

When you've slept all night in a warm bed, sometimes
You'll find a punky fragrance in your pajamas.
It's a bit lowlife, but satisfying.
It's some sort of companionable warmth
That your balls created during the night.
It's a mammal delight, related
To the cow's udder, one
Of the nouns of this earth.
Don't be ashamed, friends;
Don't throw your pajamas in the washer,
Don't open the window;
Forget the pilgrims!
Think how sweet it is
That knowledge should come
From a source so deep.

That Problem in the Family

I don't know how to say it.
We were bumblers—nothing
Was ever clear. Why the war
Started . . . or why the car didn't . . .

We couldn't do it. Probably
Some people understood, but
We just got on the tractor.
We had no one to call meetings.

"Why do you drink?" No one
Asked that, except my mother. She
Did, and the rest of us said, "I don't
Want to be on her side."

Four

Heard Whispers

The spider sways in October winds; she hears the whisk
Of the bat's foot as it leaves the branch, the groan
The bear makes far out on the Labrador ice,
The cry of the wren as the hurricane takes
The house, the cones falling, the sigh of the nun
As she dies, the whisper Jesus makes to
The woman drawing water, the nearly silent weeping
Of bones eager to be laid away in the grave.

The Slim Fir Seeds

The nimble ovenbird, the dignity of pears,
The simplicity of oars, the imperishable
Engines inside slim fir seeds, all of these
Make clear how much we want the impermanent
To be permanent. We want the hermit wren
To keep her eggs even during the storm.
But that's impossible. We are perishable;
Friends, we are salty, impermanent kingdoms.

The Big-Nostrilled Moose

Horses go on eating the Apostle Island ferns,
Also sheep and goats; also the big-nostrilled moose
Who knocks down the common bushes
In his longing for earthly pleasure.
The moose's great cock floats in the lily pads.
That image calms us. His nose calms us.
Slowly, obstinately, we retrieve the pleasures
The Fathers, angry with the Gnostics, threw away.

Tristan and Isolde

The glad body sings its four-leggéd tunes.
It has its honesty. Lovers know the obstinacy
Of the animal, the grunts that say to spirit,
Gone, gone! The awl pulls from the leather;
The thread pulls from the needle's eye. Later
He seems good to her eyes, like a waterhole
Muddied by animals. Tristan and Isolde
Love their bawdy lodge, no north, no south.

Turkish Pears in August

Sometimes a poem has her own husband
And children, her nooks and gardens and kitchens,
Her stairs, and those sweet-armed serving boys
Who carry veal in shiny copper pans.
Some poems do give plebeian sweets
Tastier than the chocolates French diners
Eat at evening, and old pleasures abundant
As Turkish pears picked in the garden in August.

Thoreau as a Lover

Dear old Thoreau abandoned his scandalous life
To live among the sand cranes and the ants.
He wasn't exactly a crowd-pleaser, but he
Kept company with his handsome language.
Each day he walked alone in the woods,
Bringing along a lover's book which told which flower
Was likely to blossom today. Well, well;
Beyond that, he lived extravagantly alone.

In a Time of Losses

We don't want to alarm the heron who's
Guarding the cranberry bog from frost.
But so many hares have been eaten by weasels;
The losses go on night after night.
Foxes slip through the bushes at dusk.
So much we care for has been carried off.
The *air*s and *ar*s we hear in this poem
Belong to the hare who cries out in the night.

So Much Time

December's foolishness, embers fall, tempters
Fly up into the dreamt palace. Things move so
Slowly in the soul. It must be that we've
Already been grieving for a hundred years.
Old men and women know how much time
Can go by while praying. Let's not try
To cheer each other up. It's all right.
We can stay in grieving another hundred years.

The Grackles

Grackles stroll about on the black floor of sorrow.
Rabbis robed in saffron feed them
Minnow bread. . . . They come to meet you.
Moses and his black wife walk like birds
And dance. Among the stalks of timothy grass
The saddled horses drink from sorrow tanks.
But the grackles' toes are springy—they walk
Over the footprints the dreamer made last night.

The Turtle's Eggs

Climbing on shore to give her brood a home,
She gathers each day bits of primitive hay.
Open to the phases of the moon, she slowly
Piles her leathery eggs at pale midnight.
After hours she laboriously leaves her eggs
On the beach, covers them with gleaming sand.
Many are lost, but a few of the young
Find their way to the protective sea.

For the Old Gnostics

The Fathers put their trust in the end of the world
And they were wrong. The Gnostics were right and not
Right. Dragons copulate with their knobby tails.
Some somnolent wealth rises unconcerned,
Yes, over there! Ponderous stubborn
Sorrow weighs down the flying Gospels.
Scholars cobble together new versions.
The untempered soul grumbles in empty light.

The Pheasant Chicks

"As soon as the master is untied, the bird soars."
That is what Tao Yuanming said one day.
"In the sad heat of noon the pheasant chicks
Spread their new wings in the moon dust."
So many body cells recognize their loneliness.
Laughter goes back to the roots of trees.
When I put myself last, an old sorrow comes.
An old sadness returns in the sorrowing dust.

Orion and the Farmstead

Orion, that old hunter, floats among the stars
Firmly . . . the farms beneath his feet. How long
It takes for me to agree to walk like him.
Eighty years old, and still placing my feet
So hopefully each night on the ground.
It takes a long time to agree to sorrow.
But that great walker follows his dogs,
Hunting all night among the disappearing stars.

Silent in the Moonlight

Silent in the moonlight, no beginning or end.
Alone, and not alone. A man and a woman lie
On open ground, under an antelope robe.
They sleep under animal skin, looking up
At the old, clear stars. How many years?
The robe thrown over them, rough
Where they sleep. Outside, the moon, the plains
Silent in the moonlight, no beginning or end.

A Ramage for the Mountain

Silent in the moonlight, no beginning or end.
So the binding things are lost, then found again,
The tines dug out of the snow, the singing so low
The other cannot hear it. Some sounds do fit
Thick cords and strong fingers. Slowly the mountain
Enters the man who walks on its slopes alone.
He walks, he sits down, he finds a stone;
No one has seen it, he sits down and is alone.

What Is Sorrow For?

What is sorrow for? It is a storehouse
Where we store wheat, barley, corn and tears.
We step to the door on a round stone,
And the storehouse feeds all the birds of sorrow.
And I say to myself: Will you have
Sorrow at last? Go on, be cheerful in autumn,
Be stoic, yes, be tranquil, calm;
Or in the valley of sorrows spread your wings.

Lovers in the River

Peony blossoms open in starlight. The lovers
Cross the river carefully, secretly, secretly.
All night horses stamp on the sandy island.
Husbands feel uneasy tonight; their wives,
We know, have gathered with Krishna in the river,
Their bodies sweetened by glad bones.
While David sings, stars fall into the sea; Uriah
Dies . . . It is the madness of the dark-faced God.

The Camels

So many camels kneel to take their burdens on.
What choice do we have but to go down? How
Can I be close to you if I'm not sad? The clam tumbles
In the surf, and amber holds the secret desires
The bee felt before his room grew silent.
The salmon has to weave through so many waters
Before he can return to his old home.
So many stammerers labor to speak one word.

Limits

So in the bear's cabin we come to earth.
There are limits. Among all the limits
We know so few things. How is it I know
Only one river—its turns—and one woman?
The love of woman is the knowing of grief.
There are no limits to grief. The loving man
Simmers his porcupine stew. Among the tim-
Ber growing on earth grief finds roots.

Five

Sunday Afternoon

The snow is falling, and the world is calm.
The flakes are light, but they cool the world
As they fall, and add to the calm of the house.
It's Sunday afternoon. I am reading
Longinus while the Super Bowl is on.
The snow is falling, and the world is calm.

The Teapot

That morning I heard water being poured into a teapot.
The sound was an ordinary, daily, cluffy sound.
But all at once, I knew you loved me.
An unheard-of thing, love audible in water falling.

Ready to Sleep

Don't be afraid.
The great lettuce of the world
Is all around us.

The Housefly

Blessings now on all
Who bend their heads!
Didn't Joseph bend
His head low to kiss
The baker's feet?
The muskrat gives up
His father's house.
The housefly bends his
Head down and gives
Up his elegant
Heaven to live with us.

My Father at Forty

I loved him so much. I've said
That before, so don't be surprised.
It was a first love. Go ahead, open
Your hand. Do scissors beat
Paper? Does rock beat scissors?
It's just love and can't be
Explained. Probably it
Happened early. You're looking
At it. The way I found
Of opening a poem I took
From the way he walked into a field.

My Mother

My mother was afraid—oh not
Of the things you imagine—just
Tuberculosis, death,
And my father. She did all right.

There was some sweetness
Bubbling up—a lot of affection
And early happiness. She didn't take
Being a mother too seriously.

Her own mother died of the flu
In the First War. So
Everything was shaky.
People kept leaving.

She had an instinct to
Escape herself. She took a job
In town and bought a piano
With her own money.

She lived a long time
In the old people's home.
The nurses liked her,
But she hardly said a word.

It's Morning Again

for Bridget

It's morning again. Last night I spent hours
In a dream, and I had to keep silent,
As if we were visiting crickets or nuns.

It's a good morning. The cat sleeps all day
Under the lilac bush, and scholars go on
Discovering new maps of Constantinople.

My daughter has found that her girlish things
Were all moonshine. Now she has a baby.
She is the sun and the baby is asleep.

Something to Do for Aunt Clara

There's something we hold to in the morning. Maybe
It's just the light, or the way the clock by the bed
Changes slowly, or how wall paintings gradually
Become clear, or the good weight of the eiderdown.
Maybe it's all the books here in this room.
And the sound of dishes rattling, and the teenagers
Waking up, and a child muttering to herself. Now we have time
For the last few sips of coffee before we go to the funeral.

The Man at the Door

Last night in my dream I took some steps
Underground. It seemed to be a holy place—
Perhaps monks a thousand years ago
Thought there. I had almost forgotten them.

How could we forget? Well, it's easy.
A guard at the door—you know the kind,
Those who keep people out—stopped me.
I began singing, "*Hum-du-lah,*

"*Hum-du-lah.*" I couldn't remember
What those words meant.
But the man at the door grew
Light-headed, and let me slip in.

The Hermit

Early in the morning the hermit wakes, hearing
The roots of the fir tree stir beneath his floor.
Someone is there. That strength buried
In earth carries up the summer world. When
A man loves a woman, he nourishes her.
Dancers strew the lawn with the light of their feet.
When a woman loves the earth, she nourishes it.
Earth nourishes what no one can see.

A Poetry Reading at Benedictine College in Atchison, Kansas

to remember William Stafford

We moved the poetry reading to the Exercise Room
For coziness. There we shifted a large bike to the side.
A certain exhilaration entered the room
When the words all agreed to point in one direction.

You said that Lewis and Clark's gang one night
Slept over there by the river, and Amelia Earhart
Lived till she was twelve in that gray house.
Maybe we could all do something brave if we tried.

We, even the heaviest, started to float when we
Remembered the sound of a moth on a screen
Trying to get out. Our lives might change today!
Listening with Sister Faith in the Exercise Room.

Six

Uncertainty

There are so many worlds under the fingernails—
I don't know what to say—probably
We have been keeping slaves alive at night.

I worry about my friends on their lonely road—
They didn't get much good from knowing us—
We kept sending ourselves on the wrong path.

Each day your wife swears she won't leave you,
And each night she is gone; we have to call
Up all our old enemies to find her again.

Most nights the moon returns to its place in the sky.
But there are no messages for twelve hours.
God sends a note saying that he will be late.

Occasionally a victim gets out of prison,
And takes a room across the street. As soon as he waves
To us, policemen appear and take him away.

Each of these stanzas says something, but what?
Each line says something we don't want to hear.
But each is a stone that takes us over the river.

The Threshers

There's no use whining over lost worlds.
The old chicken never picks up the last grains,
And the threshers usually go home when night comes.

Have we thanked the sun for shining so well?
Have we blessed the clouds for their thoughtfulness?
Have we thanked the rain that falls on the fields?

It would be good to go back a hundred years,
And recite some of Wordsworth's sonnets to him.
But it's probably best to let him go on walking.

Let's just agree we're on our own now,
And that we have to wash our own pajamas,
And figure out some way to get home.

We can still tell stories about the Dillinger boys,
And we can still buy balloons for our children,
But it will be hard to make up *The Book of Hours*.

We know that most lost fathers never return,
And the clocks run only one way,
And the threshers always go home when night comes.

The Longing

I don't know why air drops gather on the inside
Of water glasses, and why the shaggy dog
Always seems to be waiting for heaven.

We have had more blessings than our parents had.
Even on Mondays, we can knock on doors
Asking strangers to give us a ticket to heaven.

The porcupine climbs straight up the tree
With his heavy tail hanging down,
But he doesn't give two beans for heaven.

The old man lying in bed writing poems
Feels his brain light up, and he knows
That in some odd way he is approaching heaven.

Men sometimes turn around to see a woman better.
The eyes of beautiful women often glow
When the handsome priest talks of heaven.

I write these poems so happily each day.
I guess it means that I've had a longing
All morning to write the word "heaven."

What Did We See Today?

Some days we are passive, listening to the incoming waves.
On other days, we are like a light that sweeps
Out over the husky soybean fields all night.

What did we see today? Horses at the end
Of their tethering ropes, the wing of affection going over,
Flying bulls glimpsed passing the moon disc.

Rather than arguing about whether Giordano Bruno
Was right or not, it might be better to fall silent
And lose ourselves in the curved energy.

We know how many men live alone in their twenties,
And how many women are married to the wrong person,
And how many fathers and sons are strangers to each other.

It's all right if we keep forgetting the way home.
It's all right if we don't remember when we were born.
It's all right if we write the same poem over and over.

Robert, I don't know why you talk so confidently
About yourself in this way. There are a lot of shady
Characters in this town, and you are one of them.

The Long-Leggéd Birds

We know the suffering is about to begin again.
It's in the long-leggéd birds flying over the house,
And in the low strings played by women on Good Friday.

Boys love to play flutes made of grass blades.
And bent trumpets keep on calling to the moon.
But the violin aims for failure and redemption.

The tortoise has a lot of trouble dragging its shell.
You and I have tried in a thousand ingenious ways
To keep up with the suffering expected of us.

There's no use in our trying to be normal.
A dozen times a day we rewrite the details
That would give strangers a glimpse of us.

The musicians were clearly magicians once.
Their sorrow goes on long after the strings are still,
And a hundred sufferings dissolve into a single chord.

None of us old ones are able to find enough suffering.
Each day we remember the long-leggéd birds flying
Over the house and our longing for redemption.

Hearing Music at Dawn

It is sweet to hear music when the night
Is just retreating from the smoky branches
And the sun's enemies are throwing down their gloves.

Music is always reminding us whom we love.
One or two notes dissolve the auditor's mind
So we are swimming once more in the old river.

We are all failed farmers learning to play whist.
We have a lot of hands to play before midnight.
Someone else will have to worry about the time.

I'm always glad when I hear that an old hen
Has been seen crossing the road at dusk.
It means our old teacher is still all right.

We keep remembering Barborossa's life.
A little whiskey fits in well with our lives.
The time of the Depression is not really over.

Poems like this amount to some form of music.
We dance for two hours. When we look up,
We see that all the musicians have disappeared.

The Hawk in His Nest

It's all right if this suffering goes on for years.
It's all right if the hawk never finds his own nest.
It's all right if we never receive the love we want.

It's all right if we listen to the sitar for hours.
It doesn't matter how softly the musician plays.
Sooner or later the melody will say it all.

It doesn't matter if we regret our crimes or not.
The mice will carry our defeats into Asia,
And the Tuva throat-singers will tell the whole story.

It's all right if we can't remain cheerful all day.
The task we have accepted is to go down
To renew our friendship with the ruined things.

It's all right if people think we are idiots.
It's all right if we lie face down on the earth.
It's all right if we open the coffin and climb in.

It's not our fault that things have gone wrong.
Let's agree that it was Saturn and the other old men
Who have arranged this series of defeats for us.

My Mournful Room

I don't know why my mournful room is like heaven,
Nor why elephants walk with such a lazy stride,
Nor why the wide-wingéd birds give us so much pleasure.

I don't know why I worry about Hans Brinker,
Nor why I remember so well my old teachers,
Nor why I keep saying blessings on their heads.

It's all right if I forget my own brother,
And pretend I was born before my father,
And erase so many lines I wrote yesterday.

I don't know why I love to sleep under a sheepskin,
Nor why my blanket seems my oldest friend.
And why I am afraid to sleep on the open ground.

Don't ask why the elephants wear such large shoes,
And why the kangaroos are reborn kidnappers,
And why the sailing birds are all Romantics.

We know the salmon follow each other upstream,
And the legislators hire their own nephews,
And the priests pay to get their sons into heaven.

About My Father

The salty stars experience the ruin of the world.
My father was a nomad on the Mongol plains.
Each day he fed a thousand Astrakhan lambs.

He knew when the dangerous winter would come.
He knew a lot about calving in January,
And how to keep the new lambs from dying.

I couldn't tell you about the calves lost at birth,
Nor the lambs who stood around on wobbly legs,
Nor the ewes who went on eating anyway.

He knew how to put small pins into those farm wagons
In danger of falling apart. He had the gift
Of trying to hold the world together.

I knew how often he had saved other farmers
When times were bad, and kept them from ruin.
He kept a hundred sorrows alive in him.

It's hard to know what to say about Jacob.
I know that he was always fair to Esau.
If you see Jacob, tell him I am his son.

Smoke-Stained Fingers

There is still time for the old days when the musician
Stayed inside his bubble of joy, and the old men
Threw cards down with their smoke-stained fingers.

Let's hope Brooklyn Bridge will remain standing,
That Jacob marries either Rachel or Leah,
And the Appalachians don't wear all the way down.

No one minds if we are scruffy and badly dressed.
The old man who is checking names at the door
Speaks only Hungarian, and is blind as well.

There's no telling how many hours are left to us.
The plateaus in New Mexico lift a little each year.
It's like hearing a dog barking from far away.

Some birdcalls come straight through the walls.
I don't know why we bother to listen to them
When we've never heard our own cries.

Don't give up, friends. Somewhere inside us,
Jacob is tending sheep on our old farm.
The angels are still sending messages to Joseph.

What the Old Poets Failed to Say

The sunlight on wheat heads in August holds me firmly,
For I am in love with the wheat soon to be cut.
Let's thank whoever it was who kept sorrow alive.

Tell me who brought Hafez out of the grave.
Who brings us news of the Thirtieth Kingdom?
I can't stop clapping my hands over this question.

Even though we know God lays our head
On the block, we thank him for it all, and we
Remember the loving we have enjoyed at night.

Tell me why the suffering of the violin string
Goes on for years, why the coyote calls at night,
And why the bird never settles down on one branch.

Tell me why my titles are often so sad,
And why cattle keep on going every day
To the slaughterhouse, and why wars go on so long.

Night after night goes by in the old man's head.
We try to ask new questions. But whatever
The old poets failed to say will never be said.